THE KOHLHOFFS:

A. R. RAJARATNAM

THE KOHLHOFFS:

J, B, Kohlhoff, 1710-1790;

J, C. Kohlhoff, 1762-1844;

C. S. Kohlhoff, 1815-1881

Their Work in South India

A. R. RAJARATNAM

Contents

Foreword

Published by:
TINNEVELLY CHRISTIAN HISTORICAL SOCIETY
2.2.3(4), North Street,
Bungalow Surandai-627859
Tenkasi district (Tirunelveli)
04633-290401, +91 91767 80001,+91 75388 12218
https://christianhistoricalsociety.in
https://tchsportal.co.in/
Email : christianhistorical@gmail.com

THE KOHLHOFFS:
(Their Work in South India)
in Engliah
By A. R. RAJARATNAM

Preface

Greetings to you in the name of the Lord Jesus Christ,

Remember the days of old, consider the years long past; ask your father, and he will inform you; your elders and they will tell you. (Deut. 32.7)

While Moses spoke to the Israelites, he said, "Remember the days of old, consider the years long past". Historical pages and events gave us a lot of experience and exposures.

Historical events show us the way when we are confused without the way. (That which is, already has been; that which is to be, already is; and God seeks out what has gone by. (Ecclesiastes 3.15)).

Historians in various periods have given their work as the best guidelines and treasurers for their next generation with a great sacrifice and dedication. Our main duty is to pass on the missionaries' sacrifice to the next generation. To do that precious work, Tirunelveli Christian Historical Society is one of the movements dedicated to doing that tremendous work.

Tirunelveli Christian Historical Society was started by the great efforts of many Tamil Christian historians. In the vision of our Historical Society, many theological college students have volunteered to work with us. We are also doing work joining hands with many historians across Tamil Nadu.

Lord has been using His servants to record historical events in various periods. We see that Moses, Joshua, and Ezra were used in the Old Testament, and the Evangelists such as Matthew, Mark, Luke, John, Peter, Paul and so on in the New Testament.

We would like to thank God for using our Tirunelveli Christian Historical Society for its magnificent work.

CHAPTER ONE

THE KOHLHOFFS:

J, B, Kohlhoff, 1710-1790;
J, C. Kohlhoff, 1762-1844;
C. S. Kohlhoff, 1815-1881
Their Work in South India

In the history of the church in the Tamil Country, it is a pleasure to recall the faithful and devout services done by missionaries of more than one generation - father and son - in different periods of its history. The names which come to my mind in this connection are those of the Kohlhoffs Rheniuses, and Schaffters. Among these the record of the Kohlhoffs is unique, as Kohlhoffs of three generations --- grandfather, father and son - worked here as faithful servants of Christ for more than one and a half centuries. Bishop Caldwell, who lived during the life time of the Kohlhoff of the third generation (C. S. Kohlhoff), has written about them as follows: "John Balthasar Kohlhoff, the founder of this missionary line, laboured 53 years in India as a missionary. John Caspar Kohlhoff, his son, from his ordination till his death, 57 years. 110 years of labour were thus divided between father and son. The godly succession still continues. Christian Samuel Kohlhoff, grandson of the first of the name, and son of the second, was born on the 15th May 1815. He was ordained on the

6th January 1839; and had therefore completed the 41st year of his ministry when these lines were written in January 1880."[1] The missionary line ended on December 3, 1881 when C. S. Kohlhoff died. These remarkable men worked in South-India for an aggregate period of 156 (152) years."[2]

The entire life histories of these missionaries cannot be be told within the limits of such a paper as this. I shall however attempt to summarise these lives in broad outline. I shall depict their times and the difficulties experienced by them in their efforts to spread the Gospel in South India. Political conditions were changing, and correspondingly in missionary methods also there were changes during the one and a half centuries covered by the missionary line of the Kohlhoffs.

1. Early History of Tinnevelly Mission by Bishop Caldwell (p. 101)

2. "South India Missions by J. A. Sharrock (p. 45)

CHAPTER TWO

1. J. B. Kohlhoff:

The first of the three Kohlhoffs - John Balthasar Kohlhoff - was born in Germany four years after the firsttwo Protestant missionaries, Ziegenbalg and Pluetschau. Landed in Tranquebar on the Coromandel Coast in South India (1706); and during the lifetime of the last of the Kohlhoffs, Christianity had spread in all the coastal districts in the South, and in the interior districts. Within eighty years of the arrival of the Tranquebar missionaries, the first Protestant church - known as Clorinda's Church was built in 1785 in Palamcottah in the Southernmost District of the country.

When Ziegenbalg died in 1717, the number of converts to Christianity in Tranquebar and the villages around it amounted to 365, and besides there was a number of catechumens. His successors continued missionary work with vigour and enthusiasm, encouraged by supporters in Europe. In July 1717, under the auspices of the Society for Promoting Christian Knowledge, a school was opened at Cuddalore, about 80 miles North of Tranquebar; and this was followed by another at Madras. During the next two decades work spread to Tanjore, about fifty miles in the interior. It was when prospects of opening more centres of missionary enterprise were becoming bright and when the mission was in need of more workers that J. B. Kohlhoff came to this country accompanied by Godfrey William Obeiah and John Christian Wiedebrock. They arrived in Tranquebar in August 1737.

J. B. Kohlhoff 'offered for service of God' in 1736 after completing his studies in Halle in Germany and after his ordination. He understood both Danish and Dutch, and was well versed in German, Portuguese, English and Tamil. The Society for Promoting Christian Knowledge, which had in 1709 begun to support the evangelical work of the Danish Mission, accepted the offer of J. B. Kohlhoff to serve in India, and gave him a warm welcome when he arrived in England en route to India. He stayed in England for a few days and sailed for India along with his colleagues. When they arrived in India Sartorius and Geister, who had worked there for a number of years, left for Cuddalore 'to found a new mission there'. J. B. Kohlhoff and his colleagues took their places, and very soon Kohlhoff was able to establish himself as a devoted servant of Christ and as a missionary whom people greatly revered for his humility, devotion and zeal in his work.

In 1750 C. F. Schwartz, who later on became widely known as the apostle of Christ in South India, landed in Cuddalore, and proceeded to Tranquebar. There he found in Kohlhoff a missionary on whom he could rely for assistance and guidance. In February 1754 both proceeded to Cuddalore, stopping at various places to talk with the people and preach the Gospel. Reaching Cuddalore after a few days they rejoiced at being able to join in fellowship and worship with the missionaries there.

On the 9th July 1756 the missionaries celebrated the fiftieth anniversary of the arrival of Ziegenbalgand

Pluetschau at Tranquebar. One may imagine that this event was a source of deep satisfaction to all the missionaries present at the celebration, being pregnant with hopes of greater service in the cause of the Master.

After a short period of steady work in and around Tranquebar, during which the work begun was consolidated, the missionaries began exploring the possibilities of extending the sphere of their work. Writing about the work which they started in Negapatam, a Dutch settlement about 40 miles South of Tranquebar, Rev. Frank Penny says:

"In 1758, Messrs Kohlhoff and Schwartz paid a visit to Negapatam and were welcomed by the Dutch Governor and the gentlemen of the Settlement. They remained some weeks and were incessantly engaged in various religious services with both natives and European Christians. They persuaded the Dutch officials of their duty to be the nursing fathers of the Church; so that the Governor promised to build a church for the use of the native Christians. The promise was kept and the church was built in the following year and dedicated to the service of God. Schwartz paid a second visit! to Negapatam in April 1759 and a third visit in September 1760. On all occasions the missionaries ministered both to Europeans and natives and conducted their ministrations in German, Portuguese and Tami[3]. Later on, in 1767, Kohlhoff went to Negapatam accompanied by M. Koenings, a new missionary who had arrived in Tranquebar the previous year. Afterwards he and Gericke made frequent visits to the place. In later years Gericke stationed himself in Negapatam for some years and consolidated the work! Done by Schwartz and Kohlhoff.

3.The Chureh in Madras by Frank Penny (p. 263)

There were at this period in the interior parts of South India wars and tumults, and these exposed to danger the lives of missionaries and their adherents. Describing the conditions which prevailed in the Tamil Country W. Taylor in his Memoir says: "Tranquebar alone, from the steady neutrality of the Danish Government, remained tranquil - an oasis in the desert. Everywhere in the Carnatic there was alarm or danger[4]

4. Memoir of the First Centenary of the Protestant Mission in Madras by W. Taylor (n. 17)

Kohlhoff carried on his work smoothly and efficiently under difficulties created by the fortunes and misfortunes of wars between the British and the French and the invasions of Hyder Ali in the Carnatic. In the Southern districts, the insurrections of the Poligars gave the rulers much trouble, and incidentally to the missionaries. However, the Commandments of British garrisons stationed in different centres gave the German missioners protection and safety during their travel.

One outstanding event in the family of this missionary line was the ordination of the son of J. B. Kohlhoff (J. C. Kohlhoff) according to the Lutheran rites on the 23rd January 1787. That year J. B. Kohlhoff kept the Golden Jubilee of his arrival at Tranquebar. Dr. Julius Richter says that Schwartz "loved young Kohlhoff as his own child, and it was an unspeakable joy to Schwartz to ordain him on the occasion of the jubilee of the ministry of the elder Kohlhoff"[5] After his ordination young Kohlhoff entered the pulpit and preached in Tamil with 'graceful ease, and it was very gratifying to all who heard the sermon.'

5.A History of Missions in India by Julius Richter

J. B. Kohlhoff died in 1790 in his eightieth year and the fifty-third year of his service.

CHAPTER THREE

John Casper Kohlhoff

John Casper Kohlhoff was born on 23rd May 1762 at Tranquebar, and was twenty-five years old when he was ordained as minister of the church. When he entered upon his duties as a missionary, mission centres had been opened in places like Trichinopoly, Madurai, Ramanathapuram and Tinnevelly, besides in Cuddalore and Madras where work had started earlier. Schwartz visited Tinnevelly for the first time in 1778, and the church there took an organized shape in 1780. Schwartz died in 1798, and Jaenicke - who helped Schwartz in his work in Tinnevelly - died two years later. Gericke, who had accompanied Jaenicke in his tour of the district early in 1800, and toured the district alone in 1802, baptising a large number of persons prepared by the Rev. Sathianathan, died in 1803. That district was without a missionary till the arrival of C. T. E. Rhenius in 1820. In January 1818 the missionary Christian Pohle died in Trichinopoly. The burden of superintending the work done in the whole Tamil country fell on J. C. Kohlhoff. He stationed himself at Tanjore, received reports of work done in the various centres, and paid occasional visits to those centres.

Pearson in his book, Memories of Schwartz, calls J. C. Kohlhoff 'the pious co-adjustor and successor of Schwartz in the Tanjore Mission.‘ Kohlhoff did his best to walk in his revered footsteps. He travelled to Dindigul, Madura, Ramanathapuram and Palamcottah, ministering to Schwartz's converts at those stations. The Raja of Tanjore helped the mission in several ways, regarded Schwartz as his "padre' and entrusted his son Sarfoji to his care, Raja Sarfoji had very high regard for Schwartz. After the death of Schwartz became to look upon Kohlhoff as his preceptor and guide. That Kohlhoff succeeded in filling the place of the famous Schwartz in a worthy manner, is testified by the historian J. W. Kaye: "The great missionary's place was filled by Mr. Kohlhoff, labouring with unabated zeal in the cause of his Master. For him also the Raja had profound respect, saying at times: Whatever John Kohlholl asks of me shall be done.‘[6]

6. At Christianity in India by John William Kaye (p. 358)

One important step taken during the ministry of J. C. Kohlhoff for the spread of the Gospel was the selection and training of catechists. One of the best known of the early converts whose story has often been told was Sathianathan. He was baptised by Kohlhoff and he became the first Catechist sent by Schwartz to work in Tinnevelly. He was later on ordained as a priest (26-12-1790), and he was of great assistance to the missionary Jaenicke in his evangelical work. Explaining the necessity for this method of work, Hough writes:

“The declining health, and advanced age of Sathianathan made Kohlhoff apply for permission to ordain some Indian catechists. He selected four named Nainapragasam, Adaikalam, Vedanayaham and Abraham; and on the 17th of May 1811, assisted by the missionaries from the coast, ordained them after careful examination. He sent Vedanayaham to Palamcottah, and distributed the remaining among the village congregations of Tanjore.[7]

7.Vol (p. 358)

Kohlhoff worked alone in the mission field for some years, doing several men's work with unsparing energy. He had to work as an administrator over a big establishment, spread over an extensive area, paying the catechist, the clergy, and teachers, and maintaining accounts for the money received through several sources. He was one of the excutors of Schwartz's will, and later he found that he had to administer also the will left by the missionary Gericke. These added to his burden.

Bishop Middleton visited Madras in January 1816. He took the opportunity to visit Tranquebar, the seat of the first Protestant mission in India, where by that time missionary work had decayed. Tranquebar was taken by the British in 1802, and the missionaries had been left for several years without help from Denmark. The Bishop next visited Tanjore and other centres. It is interesting to read the account given by J. Hough about these visits:" at Kumbakonam, about 23 miles from Tanjore, the Bishop was Net by Mr. Kohlhoff, who still stood alone in the Tanjore Mission; but he hailed the Bishop's arrival as an omen of relief at hand for his own mission and for the long neglected churches of the South. On the 21st of February the Bishop, after surveying the buildings and other objects of note in the place, gladly turned to join the congregation assembled at the little school, consisting of native Christians and Hindoos under Mr. Kohlhoff's care... He spoke of that venerable man under the honoured appellation of "Father" and concluded by professing the warmest respect for those excellent men - Kohlhoff and his fellow workers, who had succeeded to the labours of their inestimable predecessor."[8] During the same year in May, he had the pleasure of seeing Christian congregations in remote places in Tinnevelly District under Kohlhoff's care.

8. History of Christianity in India by J. Hough - Vol. V (p. 16 & 17)

Bishop Caldwell has paid high tributes to Kohlhoff in his Reminiscences : "Kohlhoff was one of the most patriarchal men I have ever met — simple-minded, humble, loving, devout and unselfish. I heard him address the native Christians in Tamil, in one of his villages, and was much struck with the spirituality of his remarks."[9]

9. *'Reminscences of Bishop Caldwell by J. L. Wyatt (p. 40)*

J. C. Kohlhoff and L. P. Haubroe were the two foreign missionaries left in the Tanjore Mission at the time of the transfer of foreign missions to the S.P.G. in June 1824. Kohlhoff was then 64 years old. The death of Haubroe in 1831 left the field to Kohlhoff who, though age and infirmities had rendered him incapable of much work, laboured for another 13 years. He died on March 27, 1844, and was buried by the side of Schwartz, his master and friend.

CHAPTER FOUR

Christian Samuel Kohlhoff:-

The first of the Kohlhoffs saw missionary work in Tranquebar in its initial stages and lived to witness its Golden Jubilee celebrated at that place. In 1816, in the declining years of J. C. Kohlhoff, the second in the missionary line, Bishop Middleton saw "fragments of edifices which time, the universal consumer of material things brought to the ground, together with generations of man that erected and inhabited them" (J. Hough). During the life time of the Kohlhoff of the third generation (C. S. Kohlhoff) missionary work, which had been confined to Iranquebar, had extended to the remotest corner in the Southernmost District (Tirunelveli).

C. S. Kohlhoff was born at Tanjore on the 4th of May 1815. He had his theological training in Bishop's College at Calcutta in 1831, and he was ordained as Deacon by the Bishop of Madras in 1839. The next year (1840) he was ordained as Priest along with Hayne at Madras by Bishop Spencer. A large part of his service was given to Irungalore which came under the Coloroon Mission. He also served in Trichinopoly in 1841-42, and in Madras in 1846-47. The place to which he was posted first as Missionary was

Mudalur in Tinnevelly district where, by his zeal for evangelical work and sincerity, he carned the goodwill and affection of people.

A point of interest in the biography of C. S. Kohlhoff is that in the very first year of his services as a resident missionary the people of a village seven miles from the village (Mudalur), which was his headquarters, became Christians; and 'in remembrance of his efforts to convert them to Christianity, they named the village after his first name - Christian. The village - Christianagaram - is now one of the important centres of Christian enterprise.

In 1843, the parochial system (as established in Tinnevelly) was introduced all over the South; and the country stations, which were till then only occasionally visited, were organised with three 'missions' under resident missionaries - Kananthankudi Mission, Budalur Mission, and Coloroon or Irungalur Mission. The country stations came to be regarded as promising 'promising fields in which diligent cultivation would yield fruitful results.' From Mudalur, where he worked for two years, Kohlhoff was transferred in 1840 to Dindigul, and Trichinopoly. He came to Irungalore in 1843. It is not necessary for me to describe in detail the work done by him there. It will suffice to give an extract from Two Hundred Years of the S.P.G. regarding the work done by him at that centre:

"In 1843 the Rev. C. S. Kohlhoff was appointed their missionary, with the result that Irungalur became one of the most satisfactory Missions of the church. In 1845 the Bishop confirmed 134 'simple folk' at the station of Pudukottai, and laid the foundation stone of a new church which was erected at Irungalur to the memory of the Rev. J. C. Kohlhoff, the pupil and colleague of Schwartz. His son, the Rev. C. S. Kohlhoff, laboured with untiring zeal in the

Mission until 1881, when he died from the effects of one of his long journeys.

The enforcement of Caste test in 1856 - 57 led to the secession of many of the Christians, who were welcomed by the Lutheran Missionaries at Tranquebar. With this exception, the conduct of the people appears to have been encouraging. In 1864 a Vellalar of Mootoor, who had migrated to Ceylon, and had there been converted, returned and placed in Mr. Kohlhoff's hands £100 for the purpose of building a church in his **church in his native district. Ten years later. The People in the Mission were reported to the contributing largely to the church purpose, and excellent work was being** done."[10]

[10]. *Two Hundred years of the S P. G. (p. 530)*

To 1853. Kohlhoff went on furlough for two and a half years **and on his return worked in Madras from 1856 to 1858. The remaining portion of his life was spent in Trungalur - 1858-1881. Strain of journeys over long distances weakened him, and he died in Tranquebar in December 1881.**

During the life time of the three Kohlhoffs much progress was made both in organization and in the development of the spiritual life of the Christian community. The church in South India gained something from each in this missionary line. The first in the line - J. B. Kohlhoff - belonged to a group of pioneers working in a selected centre. The second worked as a Superintending Missionary and Director, exercising supervision over work done over a large area. The last in this line worked as a Resident Missionary. None of these men spared himself in the service of his Lord and Master, and discharged the onerous responsibilities entrusted to him with courage, and conspicuous success. Undoubtedly, the contribution of these remarkable men' to the life of the Indian Church doing one of its momentous periods was great and invaluable.

(Bulletin of Church History Association of India -No.8,
Sept. 1965)

9 798888 151846

Printed by Libri Plureos GmbH in Hamburg, Germany